Hsin

Brick Books

Library and Archives Canada Cataloguing in Publication

Title: Hsin / Nanci Lee.
Names: Lee, Nanci (Author of Hsin), author.
Description: Poems.
Identifiers: Canadiana (print) 20210320478 | Canadiana (ebook) 20210325984 |
ISBN 9781771315722 (softcover) | ISBN 9781771315739 (HTML) |
ISBN 9781771315746 (PDF)
Classification: LCC PS8623.E44325 H75 2022 | DDC C811/.6—dc23

We acknowledge the Canada Council for the Arts, the Government of Canada
through the Canada Book Fund, and the Ontario Arts Council for their support of
our publishing program.

Edited by John Barton.
Cover image by Leya Evelyn, *But There Is More*.
Author photo by Margaret Matthews.
The book is set in Sabon.
Design by Marijke Friesen.
Printed and bound by Coach House Printing.

Brick Books
487 King St. W.
Kingston, ON
K7L 2X7
www.brickbooks.ca

Though much of the work of Brick Books takes place on the ancestral lands of the
Anishinaabeg, Haudenosaunee, Huron-Wendat, and Mississaugas of the Credit
peoples, our editors, authors, and readers from many backgrounds are situated from
coast to coast to coast in Canada on the traditional and unceded territories of over six
hundred nations who have cared for Turtle Island from time immemorial. While living
and working on these lands, we are committed to hearing and returning the rightful
imaginative space to the poetries, songs, and stories that have been untold, under-told,
wrongly told, and suppressed through colonization.

Hsin (hold your tongue to the roof of your mouth and try to push an almost absent *h* through your teeth: *hsh* + *in*) is an ancient Chinese ethical philosophy.

Hsin is less a set of moral standards than an appeal to tune. *Heart-mind* and *nothingness* are fair English translations, but their tidiness risks losing some of the sharper, wider sides of absence and appetite. As a historical process, according to Thaddeus T'ui-Chieh Hang, *Hsin* frustrates "the psychological fragmentation and compartmentalization of the West."

I focussed on *Hsin* for this book because it is the word at the centre of Su Hui's ancient, intricate, and lost palindrome of longing.

Body is history and *Hsin* holds silence in ways that both claim and keep at bay.

NL

This book is for my loving family,
especially my dad, Charlie Lee (1929–2018),
who gave me everything but blood.

Contents

I
Who are you?

Lying is done with words, and also silence.
—Adrienne Rich

Untitled

i.

Fortune cookie

The books were written
by a few crazed men but all
the stories are true.

Our childhood rules were simple.
Husha husha,
topple or be blown.

She could smell if you'd touched her pillow.
I could lie.

We could be anyone in the restaurant.
Bestest tale wins.

Don't want to hear some sob story about
a teenage girl knocked up.

Asian eyes and blonde, blonde locks. In her fits
she would dust.

Take every figure from the shelves. In a careful rage
　　　　rub them perfect.

Our childhood games were simple. I'd pierce
　　　　my black sky with colour.

　　　　　　She'd yank the bright pegs out.
　　　　　　Let the white holes sing.

Let often.
Let know.
Let's face it.
Let lie.
Let Love, the child
of want and glut,
move, let her breed,
said Diotima,
in between
let nothing
fix.

Nothing from nothing means nothing, she hummed from the back-
seat of the Pontiac, swallowed in afternoon sun.

The backdrop
she Chinese
he Syrian played
an instrument
nurse
sailor
runs in the
story time of
Mao does that
didn't he want you
to Hong Kong Macau no
quite sure he taught piano.

To adopt (v) to take on, take up, start to use.

After her funeral, I
marched to his room,
below his bed. Tearless,
sliced and cut every
naked girl to shreds.
Tore off their legs
their heads tore their
breasts from their hips
ripped in fits until
they were tiny bits
of flesh. Harmless.

Then I walked out the
door, past our street,
past the Walkers' house,
past the bridge.

Later, he let me pick a few of
her things. I took the jewelled
handbag, shiniest in
her closet. Then the silk
Chinese minidress. Gold serpent
licking moon. Slipped on that
black piece I was sure she had
left him in. And I snatched
the wool sweater
she likely wore back.

Oh the rickety wheels that locked you
to sky then reneged over and over

carnies & clowns slipping behind
curtains every kind of creature with
its own stage where you dreamed &

hid in plain view pieced little girls
in mirrors in tunnels in each
dark lurch of more & I watched I

watched women with black hair
tried to catch their eyes in crowds
somehow in reams of colour

the likelihood of her
increased.

predictable

if you know
                        from where
                        in the sequence

does a mother
                want

She stood me down.
You offered jade and ginseng.

Don't wear much jewellery
do you?

You crossed the oceans.
She smoked and raced cars.

You would have met on god, I'm sure.
Cutting soft edges sharp.

She spoke in faith.
Body marked with needles.

You spoke in history.
Tattooed myself to cinch it.

Famous bastards

Confucius, K'ung-Fu-tzu. His father Shuliang He, a known
warlord, and his unnamed mother from the Yan clan.

Leonardo da Vinci, son of notary Ser Piero and a peasant
girl, social climber.

T. E. Lawrence, son of a knight and their suspect nanny.

Eva Perón, daughter of two adulterous villagers.

Apollo, Artemis, Hercules, and the many ill-begotten children of Zeus.

Zeus as bull, bear, as husband, tricked and took countless nymphs and goddesses. He testified to drugging them.

Not so different, really, than offering a glass of wine. Sure they liked it rough. They came back, didn't they?

Separated, having not
perched skin to skin,
tasted mother's milk,
more apt to be crazy,
commit a crime, or be
successful.

He found out much later there were twins.
One would have nothing to do with him.

Passion is random, absurd,
yet our bellies want
to be led, strung along, singing.

Bastard tropes.

The   potency
            poetry
of

            perversion.

Bestest tale wins.

ii.

She is the celeriac welling of soup.
Something beaded.
Musty camper, orange-flowered trim.
Something ironed.
She is stale beer damp alley rising.
Something born-again.
She is white suit stainless airports.
Something borrowed.
She is purple coneflower dangling lip.
Something high-set, to be restored.

He is liar, lover, winged bull
with an ibex on his breast.

Arab of rubble and televised wars,
portrait of romance as fugue.

He is Chinatown, dorm room,
jasmine tea and chess.

Nothing special, a guy from Damascus.
I don't recall the details.

It was the godless purple haze of the sixties,
languid call of legs.

He was prayer-rigorous,
neck-to-abdomen soft.

Does it alter anything
knowing?

The hold of a strange eye
persistent as war—

hair-triggered hunger,
horizontal fierce.

It wasn't spirit
no cloud of bird
bent by wind

and not soul because I have
known soul since ice-blue fjord
        fissured low

there was body yes scent of cumin
thighs to lashes lips fingertips rising
to the small of my back
spinning

but it was not skin that held me

it was a mind that swam in verse

a voice dragged through dark
        honey and figs

chipped English dropped
        ghazals vowels
        rolled over.

I love you
you said
but what does a score
tell us about syncope
or long wide jazz   you
asked for my song but
I could not betray so
I gave you my body
            where you coiled
in my abdomen
sprang up
in my throat.

                              Can't body
                                    the crave

                              I'm razed
                              I'm broke
                              brimming
                              red
                              caught out
                              at your feet

                              pooling.

You told me about your country. How birds emptied, swarmed. The males conquered surrounding trees. In a winged fit, hundreds of nesting hollows dropped like commas. Balls of fur and mud and spit. She flew through and, based on her notion of perfect, of fear, made a choice.

Anything   else

                        I should know?

anatomy   of   hope

I can't.
It would kill him.

The piano
the papers
the persistence of ink.

Symbols for *brush* 笔 and *ingot* 锭 together
sound like *to secure*.

Found, Children's Aid Society Records

You were born too
soon. Long and lean,
sallow skin. She left
Hong Kong to study.
He left just after
your birth. Syrian,
medium build. You were
fussy, didn't like to be bathed,
undressed. She showed
little interest in you.
Said they were friends.
She was raped.
You loved to talk.
When you were made
ward of the crown,
she stayed poised.

Long after he had

gone I stayed small

curled surprised to

find myself

still there

lines of contact

with the bed below

saw myself run

a bath soap wide

circles over all that

skin not a sign of

violence writ but loud

when I lowered

to porcelain

water to drain

deafening

in the way that

silence

makes you think

about noise.

what if
her body
her god
if body of god
if we've got it
all wrong if not
quite what
he meant to let
her let him
let well enough
how painful
how fascinating
how could she

[insert woman's name]
failed
at times
failed
attempts
failed
[insert man's name]

Fortune cookie

Dali too worked out and out
had no faith but believed in god.

I got your contact from the nuns.
Hope this letter finds you

                              another who can't keep her legs shut

a part of me

                              still a child yourself

I'm interested to

                              take her now.

It's been decades. I can imagine that you,
too, must have had a full life.

                                 Go on, you'll have your own one day.

When and if the time is right,
perhaps we could meet?

Meanwhile, happy to know that you are out there and well.

Forgiveness is never easy, sky cerulean. Once he tore the wings of an angel. Now he darts, wide-eyed, grasping for ladder. Rungs spin, limbs flail, azure angels scramble to lift him.

This is bullshit.
Why can't we have one?
We're working professionals.
We have two cars.
We would be such good parents.

Eventually, she tried therapy. He was a Jungian analyst, formerly a chef. Beetroot jelly and spinach foam. Seemed to take a clear view to form. She wanted to talk about this, about him, but he wasn't supposed to share.

No one else can feed your inner child, he explained.

But mothers don't give up their young without violence. This is not the tale of the abandoned girl who goes on to lead and rebel. When the angels were asleep, a pack of boys stuck a rag down her throat, herded her into the back of a truck.

He offered the various archetypes of Child: deserted, orphaned, magical, divine.

You may bypass the family, go straight to tribe.

On the eighth day, He noticed that a child was missing.

iii.

Fortune cookie

This fence is made of hubcaps
laughing at history
sounding in storms.

Orange & blue
chipped on a rusted railing

orange scream of lichen
on wood

nothing unique
becoming accident

where will you be

can poetry
can special save us.

A little move

     closer to dream

forest without story

     not in this house

slate attempts

     to afford my family.

                                  I didn't lie
                            I was a midwife
                        I said I delivered you.

He played piano
beautifully drove
a cab for a while
when he first came
they often do that
you know drive taxis.

Tale of two brothers
an artist in exile
a decorated comrade
indigo on rice paper
military garb
too close they said
to the Japanese
every bone exhumed
from State burial grounds.

His fingers plucked the ancient *guqin*
narrow throat of phoenix   zither purr

his notes wandered in a wide rhythm
each a room opening before him

his hand received the silence of the
silk string   this is the sound of sound

what the vibrations he felt are looking for
white white memory   the sound of space.

Birth the
first shame

      when past souls

cleave
      strung from
      the gut of a sheep
      & restraint.

The note leans.

              Wu from which

              all things appear

              into which someone
              will break you
              open.

A young boy
told me if
you have zero
& take one away
it starts all over again
in a dark place.

True story.

Neither rigid nor collapsed.

Fortune cookie

Strengthen your back leg
      it is still your orientation
then again
you are what you eat.

He slept in church and cycled to fires. The gods didn't mind because he fed the animals, cleaned their cages.

Silent, bent over steaming wok.

He stuffed the gaps with garage-sale finds. Didn't fly or borrow, marry Chinese or make a single apology I can remember. As the attic filled, we threw out the junk.

But now I recognize a man who can make himself comfortable.

Eccentric, or as they say of those with no money, odd. Simply hung up the phone when he had nothing left to say.

When I came from meeting my birth mom, he asked, So, was she good lookin'?

He was nervous
he asked
us to hide them
you were asking a lot of questions.

They are having an affair without body

longhand letter by careful letter   on top of the tree
shaking branches   hoping to spill some fruit
how to hunt for the heavy

                              tap metallic

get beyond the shell to the fleshy bits   spread and smack the rind
                                        eject the arils.

Take time.

In single file, they make the long climb out of the shadows. Will they
outwalk appetite?

Will the small flickering light at the end reach her tongue? Hot-
winged moth on the back of her neck. Dry copper mouth. She can't
ravage. Can't suck.

She knocks at the strange seeds, a few at a time. Holds. Holds them
between thumb and forefinger. Into which all things disappear.
Seeded garnet. *Pomme grenade.*

Give us the deaths that we need.

Of course.   I recognized you immediately.

They stole Munch's *The Scream*.
Two carried the mouth and two the burnt horizon.
Later, it was taken again with the *Madonna*.
The Scream had moisture damage and *Madonna* suffered several
tears on the right side.

At first, I misread *tears* and imagined a second soaked canvas. When
she gave up her child her voice rebelled for the sounds she didn't use
to cry—No! Words fell out stunned. They flew over the walls and
statues into the eyes of lost ships. Spread out on the sea floor, got
caught in the coral. The compounded colour of scream. My birth
mother found me decades later, only to lose her own mom. This was
a sign, she was sure of it. The gods made her a trade for silence.
        Gave her a piece of horizon. Carried away her mouth.

II
What do you obey?

Pachamama

Who are you?

I am loose flake bark, twigs, cobwebs, bud scales,
tangled bits of story, fur.

What do you obey?

Raw tobacco, my *chicha*, and wine, wine
staining corners red, how it catches, how it
burns all to the ground and we've forgotten what
we came to do. Fuchsia streams of cotton,
candied virgins, a dried llama fetus. It ain't
pretty, I can't promise that, but there is room
here for sitting and overlapping gods.

How will you prepare for your death?

Twilight as scaffold collapses into flame. Faces in
shadow and lit. Each bidding vies for a part. Burnt
walnuts, fallen feathers tied with tinsel. And a tender
rage humming at my ankles.

Happy

You told me that I was not happy
or not someone you thought of as

happy and I sensed that it came from
love or something wanting to be

near it   I struck back when what
I wished I'd said was that young

Saglana from the taiga forest
walked miles at minus thirty-four

to get help for her grandma
it was early dawn   sun &

moon still in mingle   she was
four & alone along frozen banks

no fear of wolves   nothing
but a tight fist of matches

trekking tundra & carrying fire
that I'm here & words

turn me back into song
throat song

some lit thing nearer is all
if you'd asked.

Blooms

China banned the letter *n*
so parts of me are disappeared

blooms swell between us
the red different each time

so parts of me are disappeared
you scare me   so sue me

the red different each time
when we don't police

I scare you   so sue me
sometimes I forget my lines

when we don't police
blades open & open

sometimes I forget my lines
here   where the empire cracks

blades open & open
who knew this was hunger

here   where the empire cracks
China banned the letter *n*

who knew this was hunger
blooms swell about us.

Story

after Frantz Fanon

Backwoods in rain, mushrooms brood, beneath and between. We
name them. Hades' mistress, broad-brimmed and bawdy. Aphrodite,
dewy gills exposed. Crinoline-wrapped stinkhorns, all we can be.
They break into story, die, break back into story. We think of Fanon
for violence, but he was more captured by craniums. How they
spore. Can reduce a hardwood to dust. Bodies. Little necks above
the tangle   spreading.

*

Li Hong was a poet where they break ribs for that. They cut the tips
of his fingers so he used what he had, blood and broom bristle. In
the piss-dank, got on with it. All we have are the brush strokes, bold
and brown. Water lilies lifting off the page.

Minister

in memory, Liu Xiaobo

Avoid the words
Tiananmen tyranny
Tibet Taiwan
torture particularly
Falun Gong avoid
truth compassion
tiger dragon
but especially
people pig code for
democracy avoid
military gambling
brainwashing sex
how to make
bombs make
counterfeit harvest
kidneys quakes avoid
poor rights floods
one party freedom
of expression avoid
any potential
embarrassments
Xiaobo wrote
from prison
none who have
interrogated me
are my enemies
none are my enemies
for hatred is
corrosive of a

person's conscience
corrosive
Liu Xiaobo
born 1955
offline 2008.

Canoe

It matters
how the tale begins,
they say, not how lightly
I hold the neck. I'm more
convinced where it empties,
where the river
and its low teeming
beat green,
grab locks of hair. Because of
noise, because of white foam
building, it ends. Rapunzel
as water nymph,
weightless. She fell
twenty ells from the castle
and naked as an eel
learned to swim.
I've let a few lives go
without animal.
Path-spurs mirrored in
water. Treeline
often fickle.

Tones

The first tone is high
held in tongues

skins of lily throats.
Second, rising

kingfisher, slow
circled trance.

The third lays plum
blossoms, wild geese

descending, lone orchid
lifting to light. The fourth

takes the sky on its way
down. We whistle and

tunnel, use ourselves
harshly to reach.

Fallen Fènghuáng
of fish and fowl

kicks her small head
back to the moon.

Bird of all birds and
not a bird at all,

beast or mother
contingent on

the tone. Sky
present or past.

Rust

Thorax of tractor, trailer aground.
Letting the metal go.

The gathering is shrinking. Soon
we forget to ask.

Old men idle over *tinto* and war.
A dyke gives way nail by nail.

It doesn't stop here, ever.
Through bulging sewers and

guttered debris, the music stole
back, slipped on a hot little dress.

What part of love is patience?
A blown-out, boarded-up

city stuffs its windows with toys.
The derelict car lot polka-dotted.

Abandon as litter
           or landscape?

Insides out
mustering red.

Letters

after the Marquise de Sévigné

There was a French duchess who spun long, taut letters like scarves.
They spilled into hallways, tool sheds, linen drawers, pantry shelves.
Every velvet nook of Versailles. Beribboned raw silk, broad-rimmed
hats, ostrich plumes, toes handsomely turned out, young tender peas,
sixty kinds of pears, a hall of mirrors, sunken octagonal tubs. Years
after the Revolution they used her words to rebuild every corner.
Nothing is lost, I am assured, just different. I swear that I asked him
to live with me because he was the last to send letters. Art and song.
Longhand dotted with drawings. He licked each stamp, lived with
the weight of *envelope*. Digital is vertical. We have only the limbs.
What would I tweet? *There was a time when trench soldiers carried
Pound in their pockets. When blank pages bore witness and words
flew. Few knew he was Fascist. Lovers sent their mouths in the mail.*

*

If only he touched as he painted, with the same poised fire.

Art

after Jean-Michel Basquiat

Beautiful, sad Basquiat of
patches and Italian wool,
you climbed the canvases,
replicas, studded staircases
and grateful mouths, poked
and poked at the ceiling
until crowned. People
full of paper stopped and
stared.

Fool, you knew how to bare,
how words crossed out and
knocked with colour
pop. You let the icons spit.
An organ for your kinetic, sir?
Bits of body, skull and syntax.
Not even wide New York
could hold you, bear
the *origin of cotton,*
your footprints
dating the paintings.

Pure world famous and

teeth   teeth   teeth

How to get away with it,
Prophet?

How to fail others
to lift?

History

after Werner Herzog's Cave of Forgotten Dreams

is a deal we make with
one another. Shadows fucking,

locking horns, some lost
part, half-beast half-human,

hung on stalactites, claiming
we were here.

I trust the man who
smelled the cave and

pell-mell rise. I tear back
and you grope.

Skies scattered from
a common centre

displacing stars.
Our dust hums long,

we have proof.
Take this albino

crocodile smile—
white on white

beginning
to disappear.

Hell

Perhaps it's less fire.
More, well, retail.

You've come for your genius,
come to get your fill,

cave sleek, fluorescent,
each hollow clink a forgetting,

you catch your own lines
in soft blue glass,

the horde piling in,
heads bobbing, fixing

a murder in a vacant lot
clutching its shiny bits.

Heaven

They sit, have sat
for decades
facing each other,
mere metres
apart. Both simple,
clapboard clad,
white siding
lined with black. One
offers a bell, hourly
nudges. The other
steepled, closer to
sky. The minister is
a flawless baritone
with good people
skills, but the priest can
perform small miracles.
The signs splayed on the
back of these cabs in Accra:
Come drink at the table of men.
Answer with fire.
In your wounds, let me hide.
Everyone is part worthy.
Except the Lord.

Mind

No more rounds
you asked
for cummings for
the relationship
I brought you
once you can't
find the bangle
green-grey like
the seal in the
story searching for
her skin
the seal's skin over
skis gripping
on the climb
smooth for
the descent
so fucking fast
when you say
muggle me, hon,
I get how far
how little a hug
can know the
colours you've kept
between what smuggled
your body long before
your mouth was mugged.

How to swim

Harriet and John Stuart Mill made love through ink. One had an idea. The other flew out of bed to scribble words from post-coital clever. They aimed to leave a mental pemmican. Stark meat shrunk of life, stored for crises.

After Harriet's death, John bought a cabin overlooking her grave. Stuffed in every table, chair, piece of flatware, china, every shelf, glass, vase, lamp, book from the hotel room where she died. Sat and wrote about how to live. A dark dense leather of being. To be rationed. Jawed ground.

*

A woman wet with the ocean stands in the current, jellyfish pepper the shore. *Jóias na costa do sono.* Aged and painted, she fishes, remembers what it was like to swim, swallow squid whole, swarms of red mouths eating smaller and smaller mouths.

Moonwort

Black folds into mist into
forest. An arm shot bare.

One day as any other
you find you're carrying death.

On your knees in the sphagnum
humming, plunging knuckles numb.

Lilith came long before Eve.
She led her.

Now she's back breathing
night with the sleepless,

plucking ferns
by the moon

before they unfurl,
unshoe the coming horses.

Fire

after Eduardo Galeano

Etched in a log, Brier Island, Canada
One fog in heaven

Coffin maker, Accra, Ghana
Last stop

The Halifax Commons, Canada
Look up
Be bad

Johannesburg wall, South Africa
Be free

Rusted sign in the Tobeatic wilderness, Canada
Be careful
you could

forest fire

Divine

Early sky shaking
its wings above
splitting spreading
hemispheres
dragonflies in drag
over river spits
mustard grasses
tissue wings
zim hummering
needled bodies
threaded beads   azure
hyphened by ebony
to the period of their
tails   here's how
to lock   knot of neck
abdomen   hooked
riding   waging
something longer
than love   less
than crusade   a
slow spinning
blue
mouths
consuming
tails
consuming
mouths.

Stars

There were only two left:
the word and the hand.
The hand could not hold the word
The word could not read the hand.
A star chattered to them one night.
If you are right, then one of us is not needed.
What if both of us are true?
Then we don't need to be two.
What if we aren't really two?
Then one of us is dead.
What if both of us are dead?
Then there is no need for stars.

Beginnings

A bird will save us and her name will be
Fènghuáng. A mess of colour and beast.
Mute, Feast of a bird:
beak of a rooster,
goose-like breast and wings,
snake neck, swift stag legs, and the small lost
face of a swallow. Of unusual make and
proportion, they will say. Oddly beautiful.

Bird of all birds and not a bird at all.

A freak, illicit, half
breed, half caste
son of a bitch—there's
one in every kingdom.

Her rattling scream will
crack the continents
again. It will take many
years of mixing,
silting to a fine muddle,
hues not yet tried
but she will overcome us.
Bird of all birds.

It will have to do with bees
and water. It will have nothing
to do with prayer. The Roman
Empire will have fallen. We
will simply outlive fear.

Something iridescent will slip
from the sky. All of the
colours in her feathers.
All of her animal stirring.

Last song

When it is all over—the crying and the dancing and the long naked
days I will remember peeling each other's clothes to Prince in the
kitchen. Flirting with a stranger in a dusty pueblo while salsa flared.

When it slows to a stop. Death sneaks your temples, your *belle chose.*

A temple, this sneaking. Less stopping. More slow. Before long,
the pueblo sinks a little more into dust. Your body flirts with you like
a stranger. You begin peeling.   Memory.   Will.   I.
Days   grow   naked. The dancing and crying longer, louder.
Somehow   more red.

Not the red of staked fire. Not disappearance.

More brimming, hot-glossed breaks into a burning   burning off.
Friction fire, transient skins, and thrumming wings.

May be the first chance you have, this charnel ground.

In which the end rhymes with the beginning
after Leya Evelyn and her art

If only we knew how to collide
well, work the edge,
work our hot mess of bodies.

A sad Victorian victory,
we contain the tumble.

Each light arrests
a gesture, a mark.

Does anyone know
where their lines are?
How to transgress well,
work this hot mess
of histories, guard
our dignities?

You weren't the blade
that drew blood
but what allowed entry.

Stutter or suture?
Gesture or mark?

Stars cracked and
mottled the sky,
angels crawled
out of columns,
their mouths sewn shut.

You just never know
what will move
you, thank god.
What riffs render body
nights of urgent bloom.

Atmospheres.

We contain
what appalls us.

Colours abide.

III

How will you prepare for your death?

There is no cure for multiple plots.
—Adam Phillips

Star Gauge by Su Hui (A translation of a translation)

beginning	friend	gaze	mind	duty	blaze	room	disaster	end
meat	seductive	thin	high	empty	pain	far	dazzling	pattern
so	vile	some	a	one	a	some	clear	law
minister	green	a	body	cover	present	a	starry	flight
killing	wandering	one	work	**RE**	dress	one	gossamer	star
city	burning	a	member	verb	verse	a	rising	robe
face	long	some	a	one	a	some	bloomed	trust
music	naked	impossible	known	eloquent	clutched	slow	past	chase
end	season	gauge	origin	refuse	heart	bride	book	beginning

Su Hui

first known palindromist (4th century C.E.)

Earliest female
figure survives

tradition

can be read
in any direction

play

rules tell us
how to read

weave

an assertion
reversible

speech
      body

to lure
her husband

back

object
as armature

armillary

celestial   rings 7
poems 2,848

create

choosing
snaking
down
the grid

aimlessly
turning

a kind of
appear and
disappear

hsin
at the centre
left out.

Meridian 1: Palindromes and other contingencies

As must I
toppling
a way to listen

a low wet riot
took the peach tree
fists loosened
cicada nymphs
growing harder
growing darker

stubborn bud
alone in her silk
a stupor flesh

long before we spill
wind unsettles the tale

glimpses
of under-lily red
thousands of lotus seeds
unseated.

Meridian 2: *Hsin*

Characters collide
in Mandarin
stack

moon & night
snare

wings

azaleas freshly picked

a peafowl
a tickling
a cold unsheathed sword

empty
said the master

to rival desires

on the way

a poppy screams.

Meridian 3: Lotus

I drain the blossom, undress

time in minor keys while the

incident in the tomb repeats.

Grows. The fear is you can't

break the cycle. You asked for it.

The slow drip. How petals

betray. You taught me the secret

of the golden flower before

I knew how to touch. I

pluck the stamen. Bring in

my own. Ambushed from

ten sides, dragon boat,

green waist.

Meridian 4: Murmurations

I fell into her

as

a way of beginning

hollows into which
all things

beg

blossomed

lift
and bind

oiled feathers
stagger

our fallen

draw wind
this horde

possessed of its

scatter

snaps

throat
dives

disembodied

to be

rebodied

the low
scraww
craving

to reblacken
skies.

Meridian 5: Infrastructure

Every web a settlement. Every settlement a bridge. Glands cinch and reach, criss-cross. Her black gossamer over ivory skin. The creature is busy. How far to cross, you asked me once of the clamours on the front. Retreat can be a tactic, I offered. Want and demand head to head. In the districts here, they move by bamboo train. Small cobbled boards clack through rambling green on warped tracks. When two cars meet, the one with the most cargo goes first. The other disassembled to let it pass.

*

Him, he asserted beyond the row of concubines. A ripe, rounded page placing lotus flowers between his ivory toes.

Meridian 6: Horizontal

I would have   you know   but charity of any kind is vertical

horizontal   your brush on my back
                              trace of stain on body

              moon tides shove

mist
                              release treelines
                                             in planes fading

          refuse to forget
                   what can be

the past in front and the future behind
because the past is what you can see

                                        abandon

                    sightlines
                                   you tell yourself
                    building

                                        want   state

ground to sand

immovable   historic

boned

instruments

unbecoming

release

is in the eye.

Meridian 7: Fireflies

Between the choric   loosely connected spells.

The priestess is strung below for her light.

Abdomens helplessly flare.

There is a blue night sky to hold us. Rotating spheres.

Each loud turn
                        a becoming.

Whether or not we meet at the glowing

for you I will collapse into stars.

Untitled

paddle   into dark

throat   body of

boat   smearing

stars   on water

wheeling   into skies

slipping   into ghost

Notes and Acknowledgments

The quotation from Thaddeus T'ui-Chieh Hang at the beginning of the book is taken from "Confucian Hsin and Its Twofold Functions" in Vincent Shen, Richard Knowles, and Tran Van Doan's *Psychology, Phenomenology and Chinese Philosophy* (The Council for Research in Values and Philosophy, 1994).

The epigraph to Section I is drawn from Adrienne Rich's *Arts of the Possible: Essays and Conversations* (Norton, 2002).

The epigraph to Section III by Adam Phillips appears in *On Flirtation: Psychoanalytic Essays on the Uncommitted Life* (Harvard University Press, 1994).

Thank you to all of the fine editors in whose journals and magazines these poems first appeared.

The section called "Untitled" was published as a letterpress chapbook called *Hsin* by Thee Hellbox Press in October 2016. Thank you to Hugh Barclay.

"How will you prepare for your death" (Section III) won *FreeFall*'s chapbook contest and was published as *Preparation* in December 2016. Thank you to Ryan Stromquist.

Pages 3, 4/ This poem is for my sister, Tracee St. Laurent.

Page 6/ This poem is in memory of my mom, Mary Lee.

Pages 7, 9, 10/ Earlier versions of the second poem on page 7, the second poem on page 9, and the first poem on page 10 appeared in *The Fiddlehead*, Winter 2008.

Page 11/ An earlier version of the first poem was published online at ditchpoetry.com, February 2011.

Page 13/ An earlier version of the second poem appeared as "Not a November Love Poem" in *Poet to Poet*, an anthology edited by Julie Roorda and Elana Wolff (Guernica Editions, 2013).

Page 17/ This is a found poem from the Children's Aid Society notes on my background history. This poem was published in *Contemporary Verse 2*, March 2007.

Page 18/ An earlier version of this poem was published in *Contemporary Verse 2*, March 2007.

Page 19/ An earlier version of the first poem was published online at ditchpoetry.com, February 2011.

Pages 19, 24, 25/ The second poem on page 19, the second on page 24, and the first poem on page 25 are all versions of poems that I contributed to the collaborative poetry project projectrebuild.ca created by Sachiko Murakami.

Page 27/ A *guqin* is a classical Chinese string instrument. This poem was published in "Zen Poetry," *Matrix*, March 2011. It is for Wang Zhoupu, Confucian poet and my great-grandfather.

Page 28/ This poem is for Samuel (quoted) and Natasha LaRoche, his mom.

Page 30/ The first poem on this page is for my dad, Charles Lee.

Pages 31, 32/ Earlier versions of both poems on this page were published by *FreeFall* in 2010. They are for Frances Wu, my birth mother.

Page 35/ This poem is for Lidia Ticona.

Page 36/ This poem was published online by *Rattle* on March 19, 2017.

Page 38/ The first part of the poem is for Maggy Burns.

Page 41/ An earlier version of this poem was published in *The City Series: Number Five (Halifax), ed. Chantelle Rideout* (Frog Hollow Press, 2016).

Pages 42, 43/ An earlier version of this poem was published in "Zen Poetry," *Matrix*, March 2011.

Page 45/ An earlier version of this poem was published in the *Literary Review of Canada*, December 2010. It is for Jock Sloat.

Pages 46, 47/ This poem is for Phanuel Antwi.

Page 50/ This poem is for Andrew Robertson.

Page 51/ This poem is in loving memory of Kim Truchan.

Page 52/ "Jóias na costa do sono" means "jewels on the sleeping coast" in Portuguese.

Page 55/ An earlier version of this poem was published by *The Antigonish Review*, August, 2007. It is for Jen Graham.

Page 56/ This poem was published in *This Magazine*, October 2012.

Page 57/ Fènghuáng is a Chinese mythological bird. An earlier version of this poem was published in *Matrix*, March 2011.

Page 59/ This poem was published in *GUSH: Menstrual Manifesto for our Times* (Frontenac House, 2018). The italicized words at the start of the poem are taken from Gwendolyn MacEwen's poem of the same name, "Late Song."

Pages 60, 61/ This poem was published in Leya Evelyn's 2018 exhibit catalogue for her art show, *Things you need to know*. This poem is for Leya. It was later expanded for *The Sort Of* film project produced by Phanuel Antwi and Lesley Chan.

Page 65/ This is a translation of translation of Su Hui's 4th century C.E. palindrome, which I learned about in David Hinton's *Classical Chinese Poetry: An Anthology* (Macmillan, 2008). I liberally reworked and played with Hinton's translation, which can be found replicated on the WordArt blog by Sal Randolph at https://wordobject.wordpress.com/2015/06/26/text-su-huis-matrix-poem-star-gauge/ (posted June 26, 2015).

Pages 66, 67/ This found poem was made from a poem translated by David Hinton in *Classical Chinese Poetry: An Anthology* (see above).

Pages 71, 72/ This poem was published in an earlier form by *Rizoma Freireano*, 2011. It is for Budd Hall.

Pages 74, 75/ An earlier version of the first poem was published online at ditchpoetry.com, February 2011.

I was reminded that first books are written by many people. To those many people, my gratitude. I have been fortunate to work with a number of talented mentors and muses, each who contributed to this work. Thanks to: Don for seeing what more I had to give the poems; John for stressing the space and the why; Barry for introducing me to soft spots and Alex for being one; Phil for pushing me to take risks at the suet; Alice for seeing the existential humour; Gen for hugs to the muse-soul; Johnny for pushing my lunatic; Sam, Annick, Anna, and Jaime for inspiration and loving support; Anne for helping me to keep faith in the whole book; Seán, and River for faith in my voice; Lisa and Basma for structural aikido; Hugh for the alchemy, antidote, and politic that is letterpress; Maggy and Jen for loving reads and support always; Andrew for word-play and being in my corner even when it "makes no sense."

Thanks to John Barton, my editor at Brick Books for seeing and enhancing the koan-like qualities. To Brenda Leifso and the editorial team at Brick Books for their lovely, thoughtful attention and support. Particular thank you to Alayna Munce for incisive attention. Thoughtful copy editing brings you another layer closer to the unconscious of the poems.

To the Nova Scotia Federation of Writers and my wonderful community of writers and friends from Halifax and Banff.

For the lovely space to write, both physical and financial, my thanks to EastEnd Arts Council (Wallace Stegner House), Banff Centre for Arts and Creativity's Writing Studio, and the Nova Scotia Talent Trust.

Nanci Lee (she/her) is a Syrian-Chinese poet and educator based in Mi'kma'ki (Nova Scotia), the unceded, unsurrendered territory of the Mi'kmaq. When not writing or playing outdoors, Nanci works for Tatamagouche Centre, a spiritual and justice-oriented retreat centre focussed on learning, gathering, personal and collective liberation. Nanci's work has appeared in *Contemporary Verse 2*, *The Malahat Review*, *Matrix Magazine*, *The Antigonish Review*, *The Literary Review of Canada*, *The Fiddlehead*, *Rattle Magazine*, *This Magazine* and various anthologies. *Hsin* is her first trade-length book. The chapbooks *Preparation* (FreeFall, short-listed for the bpNichol Chapbook Award), and *Hsin* (Thee Hellbox Press) are contained in this book.